JOURNALLING THROUGH
LUKE

WITH
THE DEVOTED COLLECTIVE

The Devoted Collective
Auckland, New Zealand
www.thedevotedcollective.org

© Copyright 2021 The Devoted Collective Ltd. All rights reserved.

ISBN: 978-1-7386079-0-7

No portion of this book may be reproduced, stored in a retrieval system or transmitted in any form or by any means—electronic, mechanical, photocopy, recording or otherwise— except for brief quotations in printed reviews of promotion, without prior written permission from the author. All text in bold or in parentheses are the author's own.

Unless otherwise noted, all Scripture is taken from the New International Version®, NIV®. Copyright © 1973, 1978, 1984, 2011 by Biblica, Inc.™ Used by permission of Zondervan. All rights reserved worldwide.

Cover design by Holly Robertson of Design by Rocket www.designbyrocket.com
Book Illustrations by Audrey Powell, @audreypowell_design on Instagram
Compiled and edited by Aimée Walker

Cataloguing in Publishing Data Title: Reading Through Genesis
Author: The Devoted Collective
Subjects: Devotions, Christian life, Spirituality

A copy of this title is held at the National Library of New Zealand

Because of God's tender mercy,

the morning light from heaven is about to break upon us,

to give light to those who sit in darkness and in the shadow of death,

and to guide us to the path of peace.

Luke 1:78-79 (NLT)

The story of Luke is the story of a promise fulfilled. Line after line drips with the realisation of Old Testament prophecy as he points us to the One who has come to shine the light of Heaven on us and guide us back to the path of peace. His is a carefully considered historical account, penned that we might know the certainty of all that we have been taught about Jesus—that we might have unwavering confidence in His worthiness and be compelled to give Him our all.

With vivid imagery, Luke brings a rich cast of characters to life, transporting us to their homes and gathering us around their tables to join their conversations so that we might witness Jesus in action and understand the nature of the Kingdom He is ushering in. A Kingdom marked by humility and servanthood; a Kingdom where room is made for all who desire to come.

It is our prayer that as you journal your way through Luke with us, your understanding of Scripture will be expanded and enriched, the foundations of your faith strengthened, and your heart brought to a place of overflowing awe for all that Jesus is and all that He invites us to step into as we follow after Him. May you give Him your "yes."

The Devoted Team

Luke in Context

To help you get the most out of your study of Luke, we've compiled some background notes and tips for using this journal. Anchoring your observations in the correct historical and Scriptural context will enrich what you take away from your time in the Word and help you to build a solid theological foundation.

AUTHORSHIP

It is largely accepted in popular and early church traditions that the books of Luke and Acts are both written by Luke, a physician and sometime companion of the Apostle Paul. Although he does not explicitly name himself in either, he does include himself in some of the narratives of Acts, adopting the tone of 'we' (16:10-18; 20:5-15;21:1-18; 27:1-28:16).

While his writing demonstrates a deep understanding of and profound respect for Jewish thought and customs, Luke is believed to be the only Gentile author in the entire canon of Scripture. This is reflected in his emphasis that the message of salvation is not just good news for Israel, but for *all* people.

DATING

Luke's Gospel spans a period of approximately thirty-four years covering the events leading up to Jesus' conception through to His death and ascension. It is believed to have been written either prior to Paul's death in AD 59-63 or after the fall of Jerusalem in AD 70, but an earlier date is typically preferred on account of Acts. Acts ends without documenting the outcome of Paul's trials, the martyrdom of James—the leader of the early Church—in AD 62, or the fall of Jerusalem, suggesting that Luke did not have this information at the time of writing.

AUDIENCE

From the outset, Luke is explicit that he is writing to Theophilus who is otherwise unknown, but was likely the patron of both Luke and Acts. His secondary audience is Gentile believers, assuring them of their place in God's story through the finished work of Jesus Christ and the empowering of Holy Spirit. His intention for his audience is equally clear: "that [they] may know the certainty of the things [they] have been taught" (1:4). Luke's desire and diligence to thoroughly research and record an "orderly account" (1:3) should give us great confidence in the trustworthiness of his words, and ultimately, in Christ.

GENRE

The Gospels are a unique biblical genre, combining narrative and teaching along with biographical information about Christ and His followers. As we read, it is important that we pay close attention to the style of writing and to the viewpoint of each Gospel writer. It's also important to keep an awareness of the historical and religious context in which Jesus lived and the Gospels were written. We cannot divorce Christianity from Judaism; it is a foundational building block in our understanding.

The book of Luke belongs to the "Synoptic Gospels" ('synoptic' meaning 'able to be seen together') along with the books of Matthew and Mark. These accounts are grouped together because of how much material they share, often presenting many of the same stories and teachings from Christ's ministry using the same order and wording. However, they each bring a different emphasis to their work, as well as unique content. For example, Luke alone uses a formal prologue to establish the historical veracity and quality of his Gospel, as well as a large number of parables not recorded elsewhere. Many of these additional parables reflect the core themes of this Gospel, including social justice, prayer, and salvation not only for Israel, but for all.

What further makes this Gospel unique is Luke's strong command of the Greek language and the way he uses it to offer us an artist's portrait of how Jesus is seen as embodying the Greek ideals of goodness, truth, and beauty. Vivid descriptions mark his narratives, bringing numerous characters to life while showing cultural and geographical sensitivity. Luke is also fond of using meal scenes to tell the story, elevating the importance of fellowship in his narratives—a fellowship we, too, are now invited to participate in.

STRUCTURE

When considering the structure of this Gospel, it is important to remember that the books of Luke and Acts are considered to be a single work written in two volumes. While each book has its own internal structure, they must be viewed in conjunction with each other: Luke's Gospel establishes the story of Jesus which Acts then builds on by establishing the story of the Church. In the closing chapters of Luke, and opening chapters of Acts, Luke makes clear how the ministry of Holy Spirit connects these two stories.

Internally, Luke builds the narrative largely around Christ's journey to and ministry in Jerusalem, structuring his Gospel in this way:

The historical prologue (1:1-4)
The infancy narratives of John the Baptist and Jesus (1:5-2:52)
Preparation for Jesus' ministry (3:1-4:13)
Jesus' ministry in Galilee (4:14-9:50)
Jesus' journey to Jerusalem (9:51-19:27)
Jesus' ministry in Jerusalem (19:28-21:38)
Jesus' passion (22:1-23:56)
Jesus' resurrection and ascension (24:1-53)

The length of time devoted to the travel narrative—and also to the birth narrative—is a further unique feature of Luke's Gospel within the Synoptics. It is within these chapters that many of the most memorable parables are found, including the Good Samaritan and the Prodigal Son. Because of the nature of the parables included in this section, it is sometimes called "The Gospel for the Outcast" for how it highlights and develops the theme of Christ's ministry to the lost and the least.

THEMES

Luke is a historian, concerned with accurately recording the life of Jesus so that those who follow after Him might be confident in what they believe. But he also takes care to consider Israel's past and to show us how Jesus is their long-awaited Saviour and the fulfilment of all that has been promised to them. Luke's Gospel drips with Old Testament references, and he makes frequent use of the title "Son of Man," a reference to Jesus' humanity, but also to messianic prophecies in Daniel and Ezekiel. The way Luke connects the dots between the Old and the New Testaments helps to achieve his stated purpose of giving us certainty about the truth of Jesus.

Alongside this theme of fulfilment sits a surprising development: Yes, Jesus is Israel's Messiah, but He is also ours. Luke consistently presents Jesus as good news for *all* who choose to place faith in Him. Unlike Matthew, whose genealogy only goes back to Abraham, Luke traces the lineage of the Messiah all the way back to Adam to stress that Jesus is the Saviour for all mankind. Similarly, Luke is the only Gospel writer to include in John the Baptist's heralding of Jesus the declaration that "all people will see God's salvation" (3:6).

Within these two major ideas of fulfilment and salvation for all, a number of sub-themes emerge, including the nature of the Kingdom of God, the importance and necessity of the empowering work of Holy Spirit, the priority of prayer, and the joy that is found in the message of Jesus. Luke also shows an interest in the role and activity of angels in carrying out God's plans and addresses the topics of forgiveness and the sovereignty of God.

The Nature of the Kingdom

Throughout Luke's Gospel we are invited to see the upside-down nature of the Kingdom of God, and we soon discover that it does not conform to the patterns of this world. The Kingdom is a place where the humble are lifted up (1:52), where the greatest are the least (7:28), and where that which seems small and insignificant carries great power (13:18-20). It is also a place where the lost, the oppressed, and the marginalised are welcomed. Luke gives special attention to the needs of the poor and captures Jesus' willingness to befriend those that the 'righteous' have shunned and considered unworthy.

Empowering of Holy Spirit

Holy Spirit's work is evident from the opening chapters of Luke as He moves in power upon John, Mary, Zechariah, and Simeon. He is visibly present in the form of a dove at Jesus' baptism (3:21-22), and as Jesus then steps into public ministry, He is repeatedly described as being full of the Spirit (4:1, 14, 18-21). It is the indwelling and empowering work of Holy Spirit that Luke presents as the point of continuity between the life of Jesus and the life of the church in Luke 24 and Acts 1-2. So important is Holy Spirit in the life of a believer that Luke teaches us He is one of the finest gifts the Father can give His children (11:13).

Prayer

Luke has been described as the "Evangelist of Prayer" because of the way he emphasises the importance of prayer. He is the only Gospel writer who mentions Jesus praying at His baptism (3:21), before the calling of the twelve (6:12), and prior to Peter's confession of faith (9:18), as well as repeatedly telling us that Jesus went up the mountain to spend time in prayer. However, Luke was not simply content to portray Jesus as a man of prayer. He also wanted those who chose to follow Him to make it a priority and so includes Jesus' instructions on how to pray and parables that highlight the importance of persevering in prayer.

Joy

From beginning to end, the theme of rejoicing is tightly interwoven into the narrative of Luke. From the announcement of Jesus' birth, to the hymns of praise from Mary and Zechariah, to the prophecies of Simeon celebrating answered prayers and promises fulfilled, to the Holy Spirit filling Jesus with joy, to Zacchaeus rejoicing in Jesus entering his home, to the disciples' elation in the risen Saviour, Luke constantly reminds us of the inherent joy in the message of the Gospel.

SEEING JESUS IN LUKE

The Saviour we meet in the pages of Luke defies expectations, boldly proclaiming and demonstrating the nearness of the Father's Kingdom in ways that confound the religious leaders of the day. In addition to the way that Luke portrays Him as a "friend of sinners" (7:34), drawing near to those often shunned by the Jewish community, Luke also captures Jesus' compassion and concern for the individual. This is a Saviour unafraid of our brokenness and willing to go to great lengths to restore us to the Father.

May Holy Spirit open the eyes of your heart afresh to behold the wonder of all that Christ is and all that He has done on your behalf.

How To Use This Journal

This journal is organised into eight weeks of readings. Within each week, you'll find five days of readings and journalling pages, allowing two 'grace' days to catch up on any missed days and to reflect on what you've learned with our 'Week in Review' pages. The combination of lines and white space is designed to allow you to be creative in how you record your journey through Luke. Illustrate a verse, ask the Spirit to draw with you, collage words that stand out—anything you feel moved to do!

Our journalling pages follow a pattern of *Observations, Obstacles,* and *Outcomes.* Start by reading the passage of Scripture in full. If you have time, consider going through it a few times to really get familiar with the nuances and details that are easily missed in a single pass. Once you have read the passage, you are ready to make your observations.

OBSERVATIONS

God's Word is a rich treasure trove, and no matter how familiar a passage may feel, there is always something more for us to discover there. As you slow down to make your observations, invite Holy Spirit to open the eyes of your heart and to give you insight and understanding. Then begin by noting the themes and connections you observe in the passage as a whole before working through verse by verse.

Questions you may find helpful to ask yourself:

When and where do these events take place?
Who is in this passage?
What is happening?
Why is it happening?
How are repetition, contrast, wordplay, symbols, etc. used to draw out meaning?
What themes are being developed?
What do these verses reveal about the character and nature of God?
Where is Jesus in this passage?

OBSTACLES

This section is your space to wrestle. As we read and study Scripture, it's important that we don't gloss over the hard parts. We need to be honest with ourselves about what we don't understand, what we struggle to reconcile with what we know about God, what feels contradictory with other parts of the Bible, and what might be difficult to implement. If we don't voice these things, doubt can begin to erode the foundations of our faith.

Each day, we encourage you to record the things you've read that pose an obstacle for you—whether it's an issue of understanding or outworking. Then, if you need to do some research to understand more fully, research. If you need to sit with the Lord and let Holy Spirit guide you, sit. Know that God is big enough to handle your questions and wants to empower you to walk in the truth of His Word. You might not always uncover the answers you're looking for immediately, but identifying the things you wrestle with starts the conversation and makes a space for Holy Spirit to instruct you in this area.

OUTCOMES

This is where we pause to consider the application of the passage in the context of our everyday lives. We don't want to simply consume information but to allow ourselves to be shaped and transformed by the words which ultimately point us to the Living Word: Christ. This will only happen if we recognise that God's Word is alive and active, understanding that while it has an intended application for its original audience, it also meets us where we are at today.

Take some time to reflect. *Is there something God is inviting you to do in response to what you have read? Something He is wanting to encourage you with at this time?* Write these things down and invite Holy Spirit to show you how you can practically outwork them.

Using 'the 3 Os' to study and meditate on the Word will help you draw closer to the heart of the Father as your understanding of His character and His Kingdom is enriched. May each day's reflection deepen your intimacy with the Godhead and stir a passion in you to wholeheartedly follow after Jesus.

WEEK ONE
LUKE 1-3:20

Day One

LUKE 1:1-45

OBSERVATIONS

OBSTACLES

OUTCOMES

Day Two

LUKE 1:46-80

OBSERVATIONS

OBSTACLES

OUTCOMES

Day Three

LUKE 2:1-20

OBSERVATIONS

OBSTACLES

OUTCOMES

LUKE 2:21-52

OBSERVATIONS

OBSTACLES

OUTCOMES

Day Five

LUKE 3:1-20

OBSERVATIONS

OBSTACLES

OUTCOMES

Week in Review

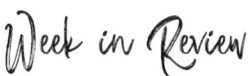

WHAT CHARACTERISTICS OF GOD WERE HIGHLIGHTED FOR YOU THIS WEEK?

HOW DID THE LORD ENCOURAGE AND CHALLENGE YOU THROUGH THIS WEEK'S READING?

WHICH OF YOUR 'OUTCOMES' IS GOD INVITING YOU TO PRIORITISE IN THE WEEK AHEAD? WHAT IS YOUR PART IN OUTWORKING IT?

WEEK TWO
LUKE 3:21-6:16

Day Six

LUKE 3:21-38

OBSERVATIONS

OBSTACLES

OUTCOMES

LUKE 4:1-30

OBSERVATIONS

OBSTACLES

OUTCOMES

Day Eight

LUKE 4:31-44

OBSERVATIONS

OBSTACLES

OUTCOMES

Day Nine

LUKE 5:1-32

OBSERVATIONS

OBSTACLES

OUTCOMES

Day Ten

LUKE 5:33-6:16

OBSERVATIONS

OBSTACLES

OUTCOMES

WHAT CHARACTERISTICS OF GOD WERE HIGHLIGHTED FOR YOU THIS WEEK?

HOW DID THE LORD ENCOURAGE AND CHALLENGE YOU THROUGH THIS WEEK'S READING?

WHICH OF YOUR 'OUTCOMES' IS GOD INVITING YOU TO PRIORITISE IN THE WEEK AHEAD? WHAT IS YOUR PART IN OUTWORKING IT?

WEEK THREE
LUKE 6:17-8

Day Eleven

LUKE 6:17-49

OBSERVATIONS

OBSTACLES

OUTCOMES

Day Twelve

LUKE 7:1-35

OBSERVATIONS

OBSTACLES

OUTCOMES

Day Thirteen

LUKE 7:36-50

OBSERVATIONS

OBSTACLES

OUTCOMES

Day Fourteen

LUKE 8:1-21

OBSERVATIONS

OBSTACLES

OUTCOMES

Day Fifteen

LUKE 8:22-56

OBSERVATIONS

OBSTACLES

OUTCOMES

Week in Review

WHAT CHARACTERISTICS OF GOD WERE HIGHLIGHTED FOR YOU THIS WEEK?

HOW DID THE LORD ENCOURAGE AND CHALLENGE YOU THROUGH THIS WEEK'S READING?

WHICH OF YOUR 'OUTCOMES' IS GOD INVITING YOU TO PRIORITISE IN THE WEEK AHEAD? WHAT IS YOUR PART IN OUTWORKING IT?

WEEK FOUR
LUKE 9:1-11:28

Day Sixteen

LUKE 9:1-27

OBSERVATIONS

OBSTACLES

OUTCOMES

LUKE 9:28-62

OBSERVATIONS

OBSTACLES

OUTCOMES

Day Eighteen

LUKE 10:1-24

OBSERVATIONS

OBSTACLES

OUTCOMES

Day Nineteen

LUKE 10:25-42

OBSERVATIONS

OBSTACLES

OUTCOMES

Day Twenty

LUKE 11:1-28

OBSERVATIONS

OBSTACLES

OUTCOMES

Week in Review

WHAT CHARACTERISTICS OF GOD WERE HIGHLIGHTED FOR YOU THIS WEEK?

HOW DID THE LORD ENCOURAGE AND CHALLENGE YOU THROUGH THIS WEEK'S READING?

WHICH OF YOUR 'OUTCOMES' IS GOD INVITING YOU TO PRIORITISE IN THE WEEK AHEAD? WHAT IS YOUR PART IN OUTWORKING IT?

WEEK FIVE
LUKE 9:1-11:28

Day Twenty-One

LUKE 11:29-54

OBSERVATIONS

OBSTACLES

OUTCOMES

Day Twenty-Two

LUKE 12:1-34

OBSERVATIONS

OBSTACLES

OUTCOMES

Day Twenty-Three

LUKE 12:35-59

OBSERVATIONS

OBSTACLES

OUTCOMES

Day Twenty-Four

LUKE 13

OBSERVATIONS

OBSTACLES

OUTCOMES

Day Twenty-Five

LUKE 14

OBSERVATIONS

OBSTACLES

OUTCOMES

Week in Review

WHAT CHARACTERISTICS OF GOD WERE HIGHLIGHTED FOR YOU THIS WEEK?

HOW DID THE LORD ENCOURAGE AND CHALLENGE YOU THROUGH THIS WEEK'S READING?

WHICH OF YOUR 'OUTCOMES' IS GOD INVITING YOU TO PRIORITISE IN THE WEEK AHEAD? WHAT IS YOUR PART IN OUTWORKING IT?

WEEK SIX
LUKE 15-19:27

Day Twenty-Six

LUKE 15

OBSERVATIONS

OBSTACLES

OUTCOMES

Day Twenty-Seven

LUKE 16

OBSERVATIONS

OBSTACLES

OUTCOMES

Day Twenty-Eight

LUKE 17

OBSERVATIONS

OBSTACLES

OUTCOMES

Day Twenty-Nine

LUKE 18:1-34

OBSERVATIONS

OBSTACLES

OUTCOMES

Day Thirty

LUKE 18:35–19:27

OBSERVATIONS

OBSTACLES

OUTCOMES

Week in Review

WHAT CHARACTERISTICS OF GOD WERE HIGHLIGHTED FOR YOU THIS WEEK?

HOW DID THE LORD ENCOURAGE AND CHALLENGE YOU THROUGH THIS WEEK'S READING?

WHICH OF YOUR 'OUTCOMES' IS GOD INVITING YOU TO PRIORITISE IN THE WEEK AHEAD? WHAT IS YOUR PART IN OUTWORKING IT?

WEEK SEVEN
LUKE 19:28–22:38

Day Thirty-One

LUKE 19:28-48

OBSERVATIONS

OBSTACLES

OUTCOMES

Day Thirty-Two

LUKE 20:1-26

OBSERVATIONS

OBSTACLES

OUTCOMES

Day Thirty-Three

LUKE 20:27-21:4

OBSERVATIONS

OBSTACLES

OUTCOMES

Day Thirty-Four

LUKE 21:5-38

OBSERVATIONS

OBSTACLES

OUTCOMES

Day Thirty-Five

LUKE 22:1-38

OBSERVATIONS

OBSTACLES

OUTCOMES

Week in Review

WHAT CHARACTERISTICS OF GOD WERE HIGHLIGHTED FOR YOU THIS WEEK?

HOW DID THE LORD ENCOURAGE AND CHALLENGE YOU THROUGH THIS WEEK'S READING?

WHICH OF YOUR 'OUTCOMES' IS GOD INVITING YOU TO PRIORITISE IN THE WEEK AHEAD? WHAT IS YOUR PART IN OUTWORKING IT?

WEEK EIGHT
LUKE 22:39-24

Day Thirty-Six

LUKE 22:39-65

OBSERVATIONS

OBSTACLES

OUTCOMES

Day Thirty-Seven

LUKE 22:66-23:25

OBSERVATIONS

OBSTACLES

OUTCOMES

Day Thirty-Eight

LUKE 23:26-56

OBSERVATIONS

OBSTACLES

OUTCOMES

Day Thirty-Nine

LUKE 24:1-35

OBSERVATIONS

OBSTACLES

OUTCOMES

LUKE 24:36-53

OBSERVATIONS

OBSTACLES

OUTCOMES

Week in Review

WHAT CHARACTERISTICS OF GOD WERE HIGHLIGHTED FOR YOU THIS WEEK?

HOW DID THE LORD ENCOURAGE AND CHALLENGE YOU THROUGH THIS WEEK'S READING?

WHICH OF YOUR 'OUTCOMES' IS GOD INVITING YOU TO PRIORITISE IN THE WEEK AHEAD? WHAT IS YOUR PART IN OUTWORKING IT?

About the Devoted Collective

Our vision is simple: to wholeheartedly pursue the 'more' of God together.

This looks like serving God with wholehearted devotion, fulfilling the command Christ gave us to love the Lord with all our heart, soul, and mind (Matthew 22:37).

We want to love God with all that we are right where we are. In order to do that, The Devoted Collective is anchored in three core disciplines modelled for us in Acts 2:42: devotion to the Word, to community, and to prayer. It is our heart's desire that, through committing to these practices with us, you will experience the richness of all God intends for your life as you come to know Him more intimately.

The more we know God, the more we can't help but love Him; and the more we love Him, the more we'll desire to partner with Him to establish it on earth as it is in Heaven. And that's what wholehearted devotion is all about. It's about living into the MORE of God.

Connect with us:

Website: www.thedevotedcollective.org
Socials: @thedevotedcollective

Join Us in The Devoted Community

We want to invite you to be part of The Devoted Community.

A curated online space hosted by Elim accredited Pastor Aimée Walker and Go + Tell Gals Certified Coach and Pastor, Em Tyler, The Devoted Community is an intentional discipleship hub away from the busyness and stress of social media, that will equip, empower, and release you into all that God has for you and help you build a resilient relationship with your God. It's where you'll find a company of women to cheer you on and a toolkit of resources to help you grow and go deeper with God.

WITHIN OUR COMMUNITY YOU WILL FIND:

Bible reading plans
Interviews & Teaching videos
Prayer threads and small groups
Dedicated mentors and monthly lives with Aimée and Emily
Exclusive content
Access to our digital courses
Downloadable study guides & journals
Believers seeking the heart of God—just like you

WHO IS IT FOR?

If you are hungry and thirsty for more of Jesus. . .
If you desire to go deeper in your faith. . .
If you want to take hold of all the promises of God. . .
If you yearn for your faith to make a difference every day. . .
If you long to enjoy Him all the days of your life. . .
If you are looking for others who feel the same. . .

. . .then The Devoted Community is for you.

Let's pursue the MORE of God together:

www.thedevotedcollective.org/community

www.ingramcontent.com/pod-product-compliance
Lightning Source LLC
Chambersburg PA
CBHW071458080526
44587CB00014B/2143